The Mountain Kingdom

2000—2001 NWMS READING BOOKS

RESOURCE BOOK FOR THE LEADER

CELEBRATE THE HARVEST
Edited by J. Wesley Eby

FOR THE READER

DREAMS, DOORS, AND DEGREES
The Story of Africa Nazarene University
By Theodore P. Esselstyn

IS THAT YOU, GOD?
Responses to the Mission Call
By Pat Stockett Johnston

THE MIRACLE GOES ON
European Nazarene Bible College
By Connie Griffith Patrick

THE MOUNTAIN KINGDOM
Claiming Lesotho for Christ
By Pat Stotler

TO SEE, TO BUILD, TO WIN
Volunteers for the Kingdom
By Carol Anne Eby

VENTURE OF THE HEART
Nazarene Missions in Peru
By Lela Morgan

The Mountain Kingdom

Claiming Lesotho for Christ

Pat Stotler

Nazarene Publishing House
Kansas City, Missouri

ISBN 083-411-8610

Printed in the
United States of America

Editor: J. Wesley Eby

Cover design: Michael Walsh

10 9 8 7 6 5 4 3 2 1

To Dale, my husband,
for his supportive, caring love
and his faithful, diligent work to start the Church of the
Nazarene in the Mountain Kingdom.

To Christy, Heidi, and Jonathan, our three children,
for their vital roles in our African mission adventure
and their encouragement to write this book.

Contents

Pat Stotler and her husband, Dale, have served as missionaries for the Church of the Nazarene since 1973 in South Africa. In 1992, they accepted the assignment of pioneering the Church of the Nazarene in Lesotho.

Foreword

*Lesotho.** Few people outside Africa can even pronounce the word properly, let alone find it on a map. For those who read Pat Stotler's moving and informative firsthand account of life in this tiny kingdom of towering, windswept mountains, Lesotho will become a part, not only of their vocabulary, but of their soul.

Pat has captured the spirit of this "kingdom in the sky." Through the authenticity of her own experience, she offers refreshing insights into the history, culture, and deep spiritual need of the Basotho people. She has traveled the roads, sat with the people, and agonized in prayer for those God has called her to serve. From the humorous adventure of jouncing along mountain paths with a live sheep atop the mission vehicle to the terrifying experience of having her home hit with bullets during political unrest, Pat interprets for us everyday life as a missionary in Lesotho. She also tells of ordinary people in remote mountain villages and of prisoners who find new life in Christ and take the message of His love back home when released.

Lesotho has proven to be a difficult country for evangelical missionaries. Few church-planting missionaries have returned for a second term. The

*Pronounced luh-SOO-too. A guide on page 85 provides suggested pronunciations of unfamiliar words in this book.

Stotlers have. Their investment of time and depth of experience provide Pat with the credentials for writing this extraordinary book.

Rebecca Middleton
A Great Commission Colleague
Maseru, Lesotho

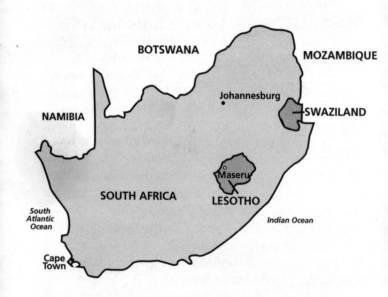

Preface

Move? To where? Lesotho, you say? These questions rolled around in our minds when mission officials asked my husband, Dale Stotler, and me to consider opening work for the Church of the Nazarene in Lesotho.

Before our furlough in 1992, we took a two-day trip to Lesotho to see what the country was like and to assess the needs and potential. Realizing this little country was separated from the Republic of South Africa—where we had been working for 20 years—by the Caledon River and some mountains, we thought it would be much like South Africa.

Imagine our surprise to find that the border bridge over the Caledon River into Lesotho was a ramshackle, one-lane bridge used by the train, trucks, cars, cattle, people—you name it. Lines were long and slow-moving.

**One-lane bridge over the Caledon
River between Lesotho and South Africa.**

Once we crossed the bridge, we knew we were in a different country. Life goes on in Lesotho as it has for centuries. Herds of livestock still wander down the streets of the capital city; cattle and chickens live in pens in yards of city homes; laundry hangs from barbed-wire fences or is thrown over bushes to dry; whole families live in one small room.

Upon entering the country, we immediately observed many beggars. Small wonder in a country with over 50 percent unemployment. Poverty is rampant in Lesotho, one of the poorest countries in the world, according to the United Nations. Poor people live in all areas of Lesotho, but poverty is much more pronounced in the foothills and mountains. Because civil servants are not particularly inclined to work in remote areas, the poverty in these areas is a poverty of isolation as much as it is a lack of goods and services. This is a result not only from the physical difficulty of reaching these areas but also from the political impotence of these people who are remote from the centers of power.

This book relates the exciting story of our venture in Lesotho to plant the Church of the Nazarene. Read and rejoice—rejoice that the good news of Jesus Christ is bringing the riches of God to the spiritually impoverished, that the gospel is truly conquering the Mountain Kingdom.

Lesotho— the Mountain Kingdom

And God said, ". . . let dry ground appear." And it was so.
God called the dry ground "land" (Gen. 1:9-10).

Lesotho, the world's only country with its entire area more than 1,462 meters (4,875 feet) above sea level, indeed deserves its name "Kingdom in the Sky." Situated near the southern tip of the African continent and encompassed by the Republic of South Africa, this small country compares in size to the country of Belgium or the state of Maryland. However, Lesotho makes up for its size with the magnitude of its majestic mountains, filled with breathtaking valleys and spectacular waterfalls, that cover two-thirds of the country.

Lesotho means land of the Basotho people. (Note: Basotho is the plural form; Masotho is singular.) The Basotho had their origins in the warm, low-lying lands of the Tswana tribes of present-day Botswana. Until the beginning of the 19th century, this area was almost uninhabited except by a few nomadic people. Evidence of their presence still exists in the many rock paintings seen in the mountains.

Around 1800 there was an influx of Bantu, Baphuthi, and Basotho, who then possessed a large

13

portion of this land. The Zulus staged a series of tribal wars that dispossessed these tribes, creating havoc throughout most of southern Africa and resulting in many scattered warring factions in the region.

Lesotho is the watershed of southern Africa.

A young chief named Moshoeshoe brought unity to these factions between 1815 and 1820, and the Basotho nation was born. However, by 1836 large numbers of Boers (white Dutch farmers) began to invade this territory, and fighting broke out. By 1865, the Basotho were defeated. Moshoeshoe appealed to the British government for help, and Basutholand, as it was then called, became a British protectorate in 1868. Gaining its independence in October 1966, King Moshoeshoe II became the ruler. After independence, a period of tyrannical control began. Early in 1993, the first national election in 40 years was held, ending military rule, and the Basutholand Congress Party came to power.

With a low point of a little less than 1,500 meters (5,000 feet) and a high point of 3,390 meters (11,300 feet), Lesotho is the watershed of southern Africa. As the source of most of the major rivers of the southern part of the continent, the Mountain Kingdom plays an important role in the subcontinent.

Water is certainly a most important natural resource. One of the most comprehensive construction projects of its kind in the world, the Lesotho Highlands Water Project, aims at harnessing the water resources of Lesotho for both South Africa and Lesotho. Water is being channeled into the Vaal River system to supply water to South Africa and at the same time will provide hydroelectric power to Lesotho. The Mountain Kingdom is also receiving a healthy boost of revenue from royalties and from the sale of water. Also, harnessing a basic commodity brings with it many other benefits. A major road that services the Katse Dam has provided access to the highlands, new industry, infrastructure, and, of course, opportunities for employment.

Traditionally, Lesotho's economy had an agrarian base. The mountain people are subsistence farmers. At the time of independence in 1966, Lesotho was almost devoid of industry except for two small mission printing shops. Together they employed less than 100 workers. Since then, industry has experienced a good growth, even though the country's industrial sector is still limited. The Lesotho Highlands Water Project has had and will continue to have a major impact on the economy. Little manufacturing takes place in the kingdom, and most goods are imported from South Africa. Also, many of the men, anywhere from 60,000 to 75,000, spend at least a couple years in South Africa in the mines or other employment to support their families. This only adds to the breakdown of the family units and the ensuing social problems.

Many young men, hoping to be hired by South African companies, come to Maseru, the capital, to wait to be called for work. All this has led to a greatly increased crime rate in and around this city.

The Basotho take great pride in their country. The flag of Lesotho in white, blue, and green is based on the traditional motto of Lesotho—Khotso-Pula-Nala—meaning "peace, rain, and abundance." The population of the country is approximately 2 million. Even though two-thirds of the country is mountainous, only one-third of its people live in the mountains.

The majestic mountains of Lesotho.

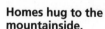
Homes hug to the mountainside.

The People of the Mountain Kingdom

The LORD God formed the man from the dust of the ground and breathed into his nostrils the breath of life, and the man became a living being (Gen. 2:7).

Beyond the breathtaking splendor of the mountains are the beautiful people. People who have almost been forgotten. People with hopes and fears. People with an impressive history. People who need to hear the good news of Jesus Christ. There are still many people, approximately 700,000, hidden in the mountains who need to be reached with the gospel.

The mountain people live an austere life, eking out a sparse living either as subsistence farmers or shepherds. The homes are small huts of either stone or wattle, sticks and reeds with grass roofs. Whole families live in one or two small, one-room huts. The winters are bitterly cold with wind, ice, and snow. Each year many deaths result from cold and exposure.

Trees are scarce in the entire country, so the people gather little shrubs and dried animal manure as fuel for cooking and heating. They stack the dung near their huts as some people would stack cords of wood. It makes a lot of smoke to begin with but also makes a hot fire. Only 9 percent of the land in Lesotho is arable with much soil erosion, which is partly caused by overgrazing. Since the Basotho raise many cattle, sheep, and goats, it is estimated the Basotho overgraze their lands by between 150 to 300 percent.

In the mountains, people gather shrubs as well as dried dung for fuel.

In some areas of Lesotho, the children have never seen a Caucasian. When Dale, my husband, visited a released prisoner in a remote mountain village, the children cried from fear. The father of one of the kids explained that the child had never seen a white man before.

In these isolated mountains live one of the world's unreached people groups—people who, as yet, do not know that Jesus loves them, who are still bound by ancestor worship.

Just who are the unreached people? An unreached people group has no basic measurable gospel witness or church. *Unreached* also refers to the fact that the people group is completely separated from the gospel by barriers of culture, language, religion, geography, or a combination of these. *Unreached* speaks of people groups, not individuals, who need church planting in their midst.

In Lesotho a great disparity exists between the people who live in the mountains and those who live in the lowlands. The difference, however, is not tribal, linguistic, or cultural. Instead, the difference is *geographic*, lowlanders versus mountain people; *educational*, the lowlanders are more highly educated; *economic*, the mountain people are much poorer; and *social*, the lowlanders are far more Westernized. The drift away from the mountains is growing rapidly as young people move to the lowlands and men go to find work in South Africa, leaving the mountains populated mostly by old men, women, and shepherd boys. The Basotho mountain people are generally more traditional in their culture, because of the degree of isolation and inaccessibility of the mountain areas.

In the mountains are thousands of shepherd boys, also called herdboys. They can neither read nor write. Many of them remain shepherds all their lives. Even though the family is important in the Basotho culture, families in need of income will hire out their young boys to wealthier families as shepherds. In payment, the family will be compensated in some way—either money or livestock. The child then joins the household of the herd owner and spends long days in the mountains, returning to the village at night. As the boys grow older, they spend months at a time high in the mountains, moving the animals from hillside to hillside, plateau to plateau, in search of good pasture.

When the shepherds go out to the mountains, they take with them a supply of maize meal, their staple food. When their supply runs low, they make their way back down the mountain to restock, then return to the highlands. They have little other than their herd, perhaps a dog, and each other. Their only education is what life in the hills will teach them: what plants they can and cannot eat; how to build a stone hut with a grass roof; how to survive a mountain snowstorm, though sadly some fail this critical test.

Although the Basotho seem to be outwardly content, often they are inwardly suspicious about their environment and things over which they have no control. Like people everywhere, the Basotho are concerned with making a living from the soil, tending their flocks, etc. But they are also concerned with the larger issues of life, such as creation, suffering, and evil.

In general, the Basotho believe in or at least have a concept of Molimo, God the creator, who brought the universe into being. However, there are few rituals directed to His worship, and He does not constitute an important factor in the religious system.

Apart from Molimo, the ancestors follow in importance and influence. The ancestral spirits, called balimo, provide intellectual and emotional explanations for important aspects of nature. Many believe that Molimo can be approached through the medium of the ancestors or balimo. The balimo are said to provide, protect, and stabilize the health of their adherents. The fact is, the ancestors are vindictive, jealous, and easily offended, and their wrath is an explanation for any misfortune. The balimo make their wishes known through dreams and illnesses, so they must be appeased.

According to a Mosotho Christian lady, the people talk about God and some know the Christian beliefs; but, in fact, they worship the balimo or ancestors. They consult the witch doctor to find a job or secure healing for the sick. And if misfortune occurs, they must appease their dead ancestors by offering the firstfruits of harvest or an animal, such as a sheep or goat. Even in some of the mainline churches, such practices are tolerated.

Many Basotho have never heard the gospel.

Lesotho is considered to be a Christian country in that 93 percent of the Basotho are considered Christians. Forty-five percent of the population are adherents to the Roman Catholic Church. A considerable number of church members are regular attenders, but their Christianity is very nominal with very little commitment. Church membership is necessary for baptism and funerals. Syncretism and liturgy have taken over many churches, and many of the 93 percent are Christian in name only. According to *Operation World*, Evangelicals number only 3.9 percent in Lesotho.

In the less evangelized areas, particularly in the isolated mountain villages, many have never heard the gospel. Indigenous churches, practicing a strange mixture of witchcraft, superstition, and ancestral worship with a semblance of Christianity, are scattered throughout the mountains.

An example of this occurs at Easter time. As we traveled throughout the country on Easter, we saw hordes of people on their way to church, each carrying a branch of a small tree or shrub. These branches are blessed by the priest so they can be burned a little at a time throughout the year to ward off the evil spirits. In the courtyard of many of the homes, we noted a small shrub growing—the focus of their worship.

Although traditional Basotho culture is breaking down through contact with the rest of the world and changes in the society, much of the culture remains because it relates so strongly to the way the people live. Traditional culture consists largely of customs, rites, and superstitions with which ordinary people explain and flavor their lives. As in all cultures, the milestones of birth, puberty, marriage, and death are associated with ceremonies. Cattle, used as sacrificial animals and as a symbol of wealth, play a large part in the culture.

The Basotho believe everything that happens has a cause, that nothing occurs without a reason. Therefore, their folklore makes sense to them and exhibits itself in their everyday life. For example, toasting fresh bread instead of stale bread causes rheumatism; when working at straining beer, take an occasional drink or your hands will swell; a spider in a hut should not be molested as it is the strength of the family; and a howling dog must be stopped immediately or it will bring evil.

Traditional medicine mixes rites and customs, with healers (sangomas or traditional doctors) developing their own charms and rituals. The Basotho are buried in a sitting position, facing the rising sun. Much of the traditional culture is associated with avoiding misfortune and reflects the grim realities of subsistence living. For example, an old man who refuses to relieve his relatives of the burden of supporting him may be placed at the entrance to the cattle kraal to be trampled in the evening by the homecoming animals.

Prisoners Set Free in the Mountain Kingdom

The LORD sets prisoners free (Ps. 146:7).

Prisons—all around us. Soon after arriving in Lesotho in September 1993, we learned that our Maseru suburb of Hillsview was in the center of three institutions of incarceration—Central Prison, a female prison, and a juvenile prison.

Four months later, Lesotho encountered a short war waged between factions of the army. For the following 20 months or so, there was so much unrest that we wondered if we were wasting our time as missionaries. Curfews were the order of the day. There were coups and rumors of coups. We were not able to get out into the villages, as it was not safe. We really wondered why we were there if we could not evangelize. We asked the Lord to show us His purpose in all this turmoil and strife.

In the middle of our quandary, we learned about a great need for a Christian witness in the prison for females. After we prayed about it, God opened the door for us to hold a weekly Bible study. As we began this ministry, we saw how desperately these women needed to know the Lord.

The women are in prison for petty theft to murder. Many of the prisoners are young, between the ages of 7 and 25. Some detainees have committed only minor offenses or perhaps no crime at all. Some juveniles are caught up in the confusion of the Children's Protection Act that makes no distinction between children in need of care (homeless children) and young offenders. As a result, a homeless child can be sent to the juvenile prison or to the juvenile wing of the female prison. Thabo was such a child. Only 10 years old, she had been in the juvenile wing for 3 years.

Many of the Basotho know nothing about Jesus or the Bible. As we began to work with the women in prison, they were guarded and suspicious of us. But as we presented God's Word week after week, we could see a great change in some of them.

In Basotho culture, a man does not cook, and this just proved their point!

We often mixed some fun with the teaching to break the ice before the Bible lesson. For example, we took the ingredients and equipment (gas burner, pots, etc.) to the prison—with the matron's permission, of course—and made no-bake, chocolate-oatmeal cookies. This was a special treat for the inmates, as they get no treats while in prison. Their basic diet is cornmeal mush with whatever vegetables they are able to grow on the prison grounds. One day the women were most amused when Dale got the tea towel too near the gas flame and burned the end of it. In their culture, a man does not cook, and this just proved their point! After they had enjoyed their cookies, Dale taught them about the recipe for a Christian life as found in God's Word. The inmates quickly understood this concept.

We then began teaching the *Basic Bible Studies*, which have been translated into the Sesotho language. The prisoners were so excited when they completed all eight lessons and received certificates of completion. We were thrilled to see that not only the prisoners responded but also the warders (prison workers) responded to the gospel. One day the head matron said to us, "Now I can see that God is in this place."

After we knew for certain that a prisoner had found Christ as Savior, we put her in charge of a cell group. When new prisoners came, the cell-group leader started them in a Bible study. These leaders also held prayer groups every evening, and the prisoners began to share problems with each other. We could see a breakdown of the suspicions they had concerning each other and us.

When the first group of prisoners completed the *Basic Bible Studies*, we planned a celebration to present their certificates. We baked cakes and served tea—a special occasion for these women. We met outside on the grounds, since it was winter and much more comfortable to sit in the sun than in the cold building. As we called the names of the "graduates," they came forward to receive their certificates. They clapped for each other and jumped up and down with joy. Some wept. Three of those receiving certificates were warders.

We also realized, if these women were going to stay true to the Lord, we needed to get the Scripture into their hands. We asked them to memorize Rom. 10:9-10. When they could recite it perfectly, we gave them a New Testament in the Sesotho language. Once we began giving out the Testaments, God provided funds for Bibles for Lesotho through 11 churches in the United States. God answered this need before we even asked Him.

After working in the prison for a year, the matron asked if we would be willing to take the prisoners to their home when they were released. Once a girl or woman has been in prison, her family is often reluctant to accept her again, treating her like a leper, like someone unclean. The Christian women especially struggle when released, for as born-again women they know they have already been cleansed by the blood of Christ. Their families force the ex-prisoners to go through a ritual, where they slaughter an animal and mix its blood with the sap of the aloe plant to wash or cleanse the prisoner. Therefore, the matron felt it might help if the Mosotho pastor and we took them home.

For Dale and me, it was a special blessing. We then knew where to go after the prisoners' release. When we arrived in the village of the prisoner, we were introduced to both her family and the chief. As strangers, people cannot just wander into a village and announce themselves. They must first be introduced to the chief and be invited to speak. This was just the opportunity we needed to get into the mountain villages.

Wonderful things are happening in Lesotho as a result of the prison ministry. One young lady was released before we knew about it. When Dale and our lay minister, Ntate Poly Seitlheko (Ntate means "father" and is a title of respect for any married

Rev. Malehlohonolo and Ntate Poly Seitlheko
and their children.

man), went to her mountain village to find her, she was not there, but her sister-in-law met them. She said, "I don't know what happened to her while she was in prison, but she is changed. She reads the Bible and prays with us every evening, and she holds what she calls Sunday School with 30 to 35 children every Saturday." In February 1997 we went to her village, dammed up the nearby stream, and baptized her. The young woman testified to the 65 or 70 villagers who had gathered to see this strange event of her faith in Christ. She is faithful to the Lord, a shining example to those in her village. We praise God for this 22-year-old woman who continues to hold Sunday School and church services in her home.

Several months later, the prison matron requested that we take Seeng Leuta home to her village, which is about 50 kilometers (31 miles) from Maseru. When we arrived, she learned that her two-year-old child died the week before and was already buried. Seeng was heartbroken. Thankfully, her family welcomed her home with joy.

Seeng shared her story with us. Some years earlier, a young man attacked her and took her home to be his wife. He beat her severely for several years until she finally fled, returning to her parents. Influenced by "wrong" friends, Seeng stole a pair of shoes and ended up in prison for four months. There, she found the Lord. She testifies that she is thankful for the prison, for it was there she found freedom in Christ.

After taking Seeng home, we returned two

weeks later and found she had begun to hold services and a Sunday School for children. The people began to come, and about 100 people gathered outside her home for a service. No matter when we went to her village, 75 to 125 people were always there for a service.

During our furlough from July 1997 to July 1998, Ntate Poly Seitlheko continued to hold services on Saturday mornings. The people decided they needed to ask the chief for a church site. They desired to become members of the Church of the Nazarene.

When we did not know how to win the people in Lesotho, God reminded us of His Word, "I will build my church" (Matt. 16:18). Through the prison ministry we are able to get into villages where we would otherwise never be able to go. God is faithful. When we do not know how to win people, He does!

Because of the change in the female prison by the teaching of God's Word, the matron asked us if we would be willing to go to the Central Prison to hold services. What an opportunity to share the gospel of Christ with over 800 men in that prison.

Lighting the Darkness of the Mountain Kingdom

I have come into the world as a light, so that no one who believes in me should stay in darkness (John 12:46).

When we first arrived in Lesotho and were studying the language, we went to a clinic one day to visit with the patients so we could practice speaking what we had been learning. While there, Dale talked to a young mother who had brought her child for treatment for pinkeye.

The woman, Marikabe, lived in a village about 50 kilometers (31 miles) distant but came to this mission clinic as she trusted the missionary nurses. She had taken a taxi part of the way and then had walked the last 20 kilometers (12.5 miles). As we talked to her in our broken Sesotho, she asked us what we were doing. When we told her, she asked, "Can't you come to our village and start a church? There are no churches in our village."

In December 1993, we went to visit Marikabe and check out her village. It was not difficult to be introduced to the chief, as this lady is a member of the chief's family. We got permission to set up the tent and hold meetings. Later, the village council gave us an ideal piece of property where we now have HaNqosa Church of the Nazarene.

During the tent meeting, 'Me Salomina ('Me means "mother" and is a title of respect for any married woman), a lady who lived nearby, was much opposed to this new church and vowed she would never set foot inside the tent. However, it was impossible for her not to hear what was going on over the loudspeaker. As we sang hymns and preached the Word of God, her heart was touched. She came inside the tent, knelt, and gave her life to the Lord.

After 'Me Salomina was saved, the Lord began to deal with her about making beer and selling it to make a living. She asked Ntate Poly and Rev. Stotler what she should do, and they counseled her to do what she knew the Lord wanted. She stopped her homemade brew enterprise, and the Lord has helped her start a small business of selling food items and clothing.

She heard one of the men say, "Let them pass. They are not alone."

During the recent political crisis, 'Me Salomina and a young niece walked to a neighboring village to see a relative. They had such a nice visit they didn't realize how much time had passed. It was nearing dusk when they began their journey home, and nightfall came before they reached their village. Since there is no electricity in this area, the night was darkest dark, as only an African night can be. When they heard a group of men approaching, the two women shook with fear. 'Me Salomina prayed that God would keep them safe. As the men came nearer, she heard them talking about what they planned to do to them. Then she heard one of the men say, "Let them pass. They are not alone." 'Me Salomina believes that God sent His angels that night to protect her and her niece.

'Me Salomina has encountered many problems and trials. Her herd of sheep was stolen, which is everything she owned, and her husband left her for another woman. One morning she came to church and testified she had wrestled with demons all night long, but she called upon the name of Jesus and found victory over them. Through all of this, she has remained faithful and is winning others in her village for Christ. Indeed, the true Light is shattering the darkness of Lesotho.

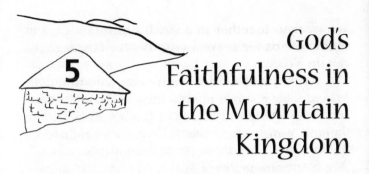

God's Faithfulness in the Mountain Kingdom

by Adanech Biru

For the LORD is good and his love endures forever; his
faithfulness continues through all generations (Ps. 100:5).

About a year after we arrived in Lesotho, we met
Adanech Biru, a young Ethiopian woman, and we
soon became good friends. In fact, she stayed with
us during the winter of 1996 because she became ill
from the cold Lesotho winters. She had only sum-
mer clothing and no heat in her tiny rented room.
When we got to know her, she gave her testimony of
God's mercy and grace and faithfulness.

I was born in Addis Ababa, Ethiopia, in 1970
and am one of nine children. Although my parents
are of the Orthodox faith, my four brothers, four
sisters, and I attended a Roman Catholic school and
grew up in the Catholic Church. I graduated from
high school in 1992. During my school years,
Joseph Girmay and I became good friends, and we
married soon after graduation. Before we married,

we worked together in a small restaurant-café in Addis Ababa for about a year, but the business did not do well.

After Joseph and I married, we stayed in Ethiopia for just one month, then we left the country. Joseph went to Saudi Arabia to work, and I went to Yemen on a two-year contract. I refused to go to Saudi Arabia, because I would have been forced to become a Muslim.

While I was in Yemen, I worked every morning; but because of the intense heat, I had the afternoons free. I had no reading materials, so I began reading my Amharic Bible. I read it from cover to cover. As I read the Bible, I realized I was going in the wrong way. I realized there is no life without Jesus. I began to see that I was in darkness, and I asked forgiveness from God.

When my two-year contract was finished, I returned to Ethiopia. I asked my cousin to take me to her church, and there I accepted Jesus. During this time I wrote to Joseph in Saudi Arabia and told him about the Bible, but he would not accept Jesus. Yet, he did not want me to leave my faith. I continued to pray for him. One day I cried out, "God, Joseph is Your son, and You can save him. Open his eyes. You promised that if one is saved, the family will be saved. Thank you for saving Joseph." I believed that Joseph would be saved.

Again Joseph asked me to go to Saudi Arabia, but I knew if I went to Saudi Arabia I would have to become a Muslim. I prayed that God would take me to a place where I could live freely as a Christian. During this time in Ethiopia, I fasted and prayed for God to lead me. People even came to me to ask me if I wanted a job, but my heart was not open to that. I just told God, "Do Your will in my life only."

One day my sister said that if I wanted to, I could get a visa to go to Lesotho. From Ethiopia it is hard to get a visa for most countries. I requested that vital travel document, and the authorities didn't even ask me questions. They only asked for my photograph, and they gave me a visa immediately.

I prayed that God would bring Joseph and me together again. Suddenly, I received a call from Saudi Arabia that Joseph would arrive in Addis Ababa the next day. We were together for one month. Even though we wanted to go to Lesotho together, our money was only enough for one ticket. So I went to Lesotho alone, and Joseph went back to Saudi Arabia.

When I arrived in Lesotho, I could not find a job. For three months, I didn't go anywhere, because I didn't want people to think I wanted them to give me things. But the Lord sent people to help me. They gave me money and food, and I lived well. Joseph had found a job in the meantime, but we could not communicate often, as letters took more than three months to travel between Lesotho and Saudi Arabia.

One day, I went looking for a job. As I returned home, I saw the gates of a nearby compound open and wondered if it was a private home or a workplace. I decided to ask. I went inside and found the secretary, who then took me to see the manager. He asked, "Why are you here in Maseru?" I told him I was here to work, because in my country there is no work. When he asked me what work I could do, I told him I would do any work available, but I was trained as a bookkeeper. When I said that, he jumped up and called his secretary. He had been looking for a bookkeeper. He hired me that day.

After I had worked one year, I told Joseph he must come to Lesotho, for I could not go to Saudi Arabia. He finally came in 1997. The first thing he asked was if I was still a Christian, and I said yes. Every day when I went to work, I left Scripture for him to read. He sat for one month without work, but I could see he was changing. Finally, I said, "Joseph, do you want to accept Jesus Christ?"

"Yes," he replied. "But how do I do it?"

We prayed together, and Joseph accepted Christ as his Savior.

A week later, we went to a prayer meeting on Sunday afternoon. Joseph was discouraged and wanted to leave Lesotho. The pastor counseled us not to be downhearted, that God would bless us with His mighty hand. I told Joseph that we must pray and see what God is saying. I didn't want to leave Lesotho. As we prayed and waited, God spoke through His Word, "Be still, and know that I am God" (Ps. 46:10).

When we read this, Joseph realized it was God speaking and no longer wanted to leave. After a week, he found a job at the Captain DoRego restaurant, which was encouraging. But even with a job, we both wanted to leave the country because of all the turmoil and fighting. We started to pray again, asking God what to do.

God told us a second time to wait. I asked Joseph if we could start our own business. But Joseph said our money was inadequate, that he could not find a job that paid enough. But I did not give up.

We could not believe it, but God did it!

Joseph became worried again. We had no business, only a little money, and we still had to pay rent. We prayed and told God each thing we needed. We asked God to multiply our money as He had multiplied the loaves and fish. God answered our prayer by supplying equipment at a price we could afford. It should have cost 9,000 maloti (U.S. $1,500), but we paid only M1,900 (U.S.$317). Then a man gave us more equipment on credit. We could not believe it, but God did it!

One morning when Joseph was working at Captain DoRego's, a friend asked Joseph if he had opened his shop. Joseph explained to him that we did not have money yet for stock. The friend told Joseph that he would loan us M3,000 (U.S.$500), and we could repay it when we were able. He immediately went to the bank, withdrew the money, and brought it back to my husband. We opened the shop, and God blessed us. Now the business is going well. Before we opened the shop, we dedicated it to the Lord. Within the first three months, we were able to pay off everything we owed. God is so good!

Adanech and Joseph operate a fish and chip shop in Maseru. It is in one of the worst sections of the city, as far as crime goes. But it is in the center of the bus and taxi traffic, a good area for business. During the recent unrest, the shop was looted but escaped being burned. They were able to reopen it about two weeks after the trouble settled down.

While Adanech was living with us, we told her about the work of the Church of the Nazarene in Ethiopia. Before Joseph came to Lesotho, he and Adanech's sister went to visit Al and Kitty Jones, who were missionaries to Ethiopia at that time. Al gave each of them a Bible in Amharic, their own language. Joseph was proud to show us his Bible with the name of the church stamped on the cover. Joseph and Adanech are a wonderful Christian couple. We praise God for them and their witness here in Lesotho. Yes, God is faithful.

Lost Sheep in the Mountain Kingdom

6

*I [Jesus] have other sheep that are not of this sheep pen.
I must bring them also* (John 10:16).

HaPopa is a small village nestled in the Senqun-
yane Valley below majestic, towering mountains.
The "road" into this hamlet was made by the village people so they could obtain supplies for the little Anglican clinic and their small store. The road is
little more than a trail with tall cliffs on one side
and a sheer drop to the valley below on the other.
Even this so-called road is impassable most of the
time.

During our early days in Lesotho in 1994, we
met a nurse who invited us to begin a church in the
village of HaPopa, as there were no churches in the
area. Dale and our Swazi pastor visited the chief in
HaPopa to determine the prospects for starting a
work there. They found a group of people who had
acquired a Bible and had begun to study it together.
They had belonged to a group called Mazioni,
which had mixed a little bit of Christianity with a
lot of traditional religion. As they studied the Bible,
they realized what they believed was not what
God's Word taught. They were eager to have us

come to preach and teach the Bible. What a delight to minister to people who wanted to know the truth of God's Word!

We made arrangements to set up a tent for a two-week meeting. Getting ready for a short venture like this may sound simple, but in the mountains of Lesotho nothing is simple. We had to plan and pack carefully: bedding, food, cooking utensils, gasoline, at least two spare tires, tent, benches, generator, water or a water purifier—everything needed for two weeks. Our '89 Toyota double-cab pickup was loaded to the hilt, and off we went.

We also knew we would engage in a spiritual battle against the forces of darkness when the light of the gospel encounters these forces. We were reminded of the scripture where Paul says: "For our struggle is not against flesh and blood, but against the rulers, against the powers, against the world forces of this darkness, against the spiritual forces of wickedness in the heavenly places" (Eph. 6:12, NASB). While the pastors preached, Dale was on his knees praying in a nearby hut, pleading the blood of Jesus over the services.

Our Toyota was so full we had nowhere to put the sheep.

How beautiful to see lives changed by the light of the gospel! In that village there is a core of people who have now given their lives to Christ. One woman rode her horse from a village two hours away with her nine-year-old, brain-damaged daughter on her back to have us pray for her. Later, she moved to Tsieng, a town where we have a church, near the capital city of Maseru. She testifies to the grace of God in her life. She still carries the girl on her back and cradles her in her arms like a baby. Fortunately, the woman's husband works in the Republic of South Africa and is able and willing to support his wife and children.

During the tent meeting, we wanted to visit other villages in the area but could not. We stayed busy every day with people coming to talk to us about what was being preached. They came from near and far, from morning until night. It was a hectic two weeks.

As we packed to leave HaPopa, the truck was loaded with all we thought it would hold. Then—lo and behold—the men of the village came to present us with a gift, a live sheep! Our Toyota was so full we had nowhere to put it. But refusing the gift would have been a grave insult. So they proceeded to tie it to a plank that stuck out the back door of the truck. In Lesotho it is common to see a sheep tied on top of a packed bus or a stuffed taxi.

As we traveled down the mountainside, we suddenly heard women yelling at us. Then we heard the sheep bleating. Its rope had come loose, and we had a "lost sheep." When we rescued it and got as far as Mantsonyane, we transferred it to the comfort of the back of another pickup. The poor creature was fine except for a couple of broken ribs and a few bruises.

We were reminded of Jesus and the parable of the lost sheep. There are many "lost sheep" in the mountains of Lesotho who need to be brought into the Shepherd's fold. Some of them are bruised and broken by life, but God loves them just the same. He wants to heal them of their brokenness and give them peace and joy in their hearts. They need to know there is wholeness and healing in Christ Jesus, the Savior. He can take their lives and make something beautiful out of the pieces. He is the Good Shepherd and cares for the sheep.

This is not quite the whole story, however, about this poor sheep. Dale held a pastor's meeting a couple days after we got home from the mountains. The pastors slaughtered the sheep and served some of it for lunch. When Dale got his plate, he found some strange pieces of meat on it. When he asked the pastors what part of the sheep it was, one of them said, "Well, in English, I think you call it the udder."

Visiting a mountain village and inviting them to a service

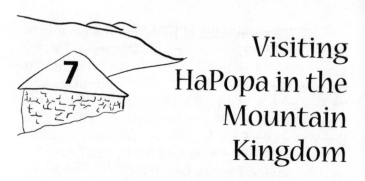

Visiting HaPopa in the Mountain Kingdom

by Christy Stotler

I have told you this so that my joy may be in you and that your joy may be complete (John 15:11).

Our daughter, Christy, visited HaPopa with a friend when Dale and I were starting the church in this mountain village. This chapter is an account of that trip through her eyes—the eyes of a missionary kid.

The tar road ended about the time we reached the mountain pass, aptly called by the Basotho, Molimo Nthuse or "God help me pass." We were 45 minutes into our five-hour journey to HaPopa, a mountain village in Lesotho's interior where Mom and Dad were starting a church. Not that the distance we were to traverse was especially far, only 37 kilometers (60 miles) or so, but the roads that were to take us there were just barely describable by that word "road." We stopped at the base of a long, narrow mountain road, waiting until the dust trail far above us came billowing past. The public buses that travel the region are driven by those individuals most disinclined to make use of their braking apparatus on those precarious cliffs and corners and who are reputedly inclined to imbibe rather freely. I wondered absently as Dad started our own vehicle up Molimo Nthuse whether this was a prerequisite for their jobs or whether they acquired such skills through on-the-job experience.

Around 1 P.M., we reached Mantsonyane the largest community in the region, which was our stretch point. As we entered the village, we passed the Chief's Butchery where a warm sheep was being freshly skinned and hung by the front door for that day's customers. A little further along and outside the general store, we parked our truck alongside the other "vehicles"—short-legged, surefooted, shaggy Lesotho ponies unique to these mountains. This general store sells everything from bubble gum to coffins, so we headed there to buy cold drinks for the remainder of our journey.

Clad in the traditional brown blankets and gum boots of their Mountain Kingdom garments, a host of herdboys lined the fence of a nearby corral. Their purpose? To observe, to pass time together, to comment upon the trouble the most stubborn heifer in their herd had given them that day. The general commotion among the group escalated considerably with the advent of four white faces in a gathering of otherwise brown countenances. "Lumelang Boabuti" (hello, brothers), our greeting. "Lumela Ntate, Lumela Mme" (hello, father; hello, mother), their rather muted and wide-eyed reply. Their eyes and conversation followed us as we piled into the truck again and left town bound for "further in and further up." We still had 3 hours and 9 kilometers (15 miles) to go.

How shall I describe HaPopa? Perhaps from the highest vantage point I found while we were there. On Saturday morning about 11 A.M., my friend and I climbed up through the village and halted, winded, just halfway up. We had experienced the effects of the high altitude earlier when we went down the hill to fill our five-gallon water container. On our huff and puff back up, we had watched amazed as women with larger containers than ours on their heads passed us, seemingly effortlessly. Still, we were 2,400 meters (8,000 feet) above sea level, and breath came in gasps.

Beyond the village, two peaks loomed upward; behind us lay vast fields, until suddenly the world dropped away to a distant river below. The village around us appeared to be suspended in space. We adjusted our pace and kept going. Following a narrow trail and reaching the saddle between the two peaks, we started toward the summit on our left. It took a couple hours of picking trails and steady climbing before we pulled each other to the top. The wind whipped us, yet we stood and turned 360 degrees many times before we sat down to rest our legs.

Up there, during our mountaintop experience, we drank from our canteen, snacked on peanuts and raisins, and talked. We chatted about old men and mountains and walking sticks and God and herdboys. For some reason, as I remember it now, one topic seemed no more or less important than the one before. We didn't hear much up there, only each other and the wind. Our eyes couldn't take in all there was to see below us—HaPopa, mud huts and thatched roofs, cows and herdboys, and women picking corn in the fields. My mother was among them, though we couldn't make her out from this height. As we lifted our gaze, we saw the great drop to the river and villages that dotted the overwhelming landscape. Then there were the mountains as far as we could see; and when we had fixed our eyes on the most distant of these, the realization hit us there were even more mountains. Scant wonder that this mountain kingdom is called the "Roof of Africa."

Simon asked to see "the glasses that look far."

On our way down, we ran into Simon and Alfons. We had met them the night before around dusk. Simon was conspicuous, not only because he wore a blue blanket among brown ones, but also because his eyes held the light of a curious spirit. We had found that to be true when we observed him with binoculars. The night before, as we had talked outside the hut where we were staying, Simon had stopped by on his way home from the fields. He asked to see "the glasses that look far."

Dad passed them to tentative but eager hands, and I watched as he struggled at first to adjust his eyes to focusing on some distant mark. Suddenly he saw it, and a huge, white smile broke across his brown face. He began to talk in a tongue I could not manage, but I knew was full of meaning. Alfons took up the second pair. Soon he and Simon were chattering about how great it would be to always have "eyes" such as these. Then they could send the younger herdboys to bring back the distant heifers. The two guys chattered on and on and on.

Dad, my friend, and I watched and laughed and listened to their wonder and fascination. Passersby gathered, and conversation continued on many levels. A grandmother asked to look. Simon learnedly passed the binoculars over and began to teach her how to use them. She had a hard time with the "odd machine." When she focused on the distant outhouse, she screamed and would have lost hold but for Simon's quick hand. Later, when we met them again in the field with the cows and dogs, we invited them to the church service in our hut that evening. They asked if they could see the "far glasses" again. We told them we would look at the moon.

They came. Seventy bodies—old, young, and very young—filled the dark interior of a hut no larger than my living room. Bright eyes looked out of the darkness into the flickering light of a kerosene lamp and the steady light of a gas heater. They listened and sang, sat still and squirmed, clapped and listened. They were trusting, those joyful eyes I saw, though they had so little to call their own by Quincy, Massachusetts, standards—my own standards. Yet, they know more fully, feel deeply, and love freely the true God, each other, and life.

I understood again that night some things I often forget in my busy, things-oriented world: that joy is not dependent upon circumstances; that simple is not stupid; that intelligence doesn't proceed from an earned degree; that accomplishment is only successful inasmuch as it reaches out to others; that God is always the end and our life in Christ is the means to Him.

Herdboys in the Mountain Kingdom

Let your light shine before men, that they may see your good deeds and praise your Father in heaven (Matt. 5:16).

Herdboys. Thousands of them. In the mountains of Lesotho, they are everywhere. You can't escape them.

Many of the herdboys know no other life than taking care of their families' cattle, sheep, and goats. Most never go to school and can neither read nor write. The herdboys are generally looked down upon by society, partly because of their behavior. Any woman or girl found working in the fields or walking alone is open prey. Also cattle theft is rampant throughout the country and even across the border into South Africa. Stock theft is one of the major problems in the country and accounts for many deaths.

A new development is that illegal guns are readily available. A rifle can be bought for as little as M90 (U.S.$15). The thieves know that if they can drive the animals into the mountains, they can ward off anyone who comes to reclaim their animals. They have no scruples about killing. Many of the herdboys are wealthy, because they have either stolen livestock or smuggled marijuana, which grows profusely in the mountains and is sold in the Republic of South Africa. Even the young herdboys in the mountain villages have guns.

Stock-theft feuds have ended in the burning of many villages. In the town of HaMakema, a cattle-theft incident resulted in the killing of 14 people and the destruction of many homes. Not only is cattle theft a problem, but grazing rights is also a major concern. Villages will fight over the rights to grazing in the surrounding areas, resulting in many people losing their lives. Overgrazing also results in much soil erosion. In a country with so little arable land, this only compounds the problem.

Many of the herdboys go up into the mountains, where they remain for months at a time. They build cattle kraals (stone enclosures) for the animals at night to keep away predators and prevent other herdboys from stealing them.

In winter herdboys wrap their feet in old strips of cloth or paper to keep them warm.

These boys live lonely, isolated lives. They make musical instruments of many kinds, which they use for playing and accompanying their singing. (A common instrument is a large, dried gourd with strings like a harp.) They spend the winter in the mountains with little clothing to keep them warm, making survival an amazing feat. Typical attire includes a heavy diaper, a blanket around their shoulders, and tall, gum boots. In winter they wrap their feet in old strips of cloth or paper to keep them warm. Woe to anyone who is within smelling distance when they take those boots off!

In the winter of 1996, a heavy, unexpected 3-meter (10-foot) snowfall left Letsenghatrae and Tlhanyaku, two mountain communities, completely cut off from access to food and fuel supplies. South Africa and Lesotho coordinated an airdrop by army helicopters of needed supplies—food, blankets, and clothing—to these remote areas. The few existing roads into the mountains were impassable for weeks. Many herdboys died of cold and starvation during this national disaster when they ran out of fuel and food. Some had used the only available fuel, the sticks and grass on their huts'

A Bible study in the mountain village of Tlhanyaku

roofs. When that fuel source ran out, the herdboys died of cold and exposure.

In one isolated mountain area, the helicopter landed and the pilot asked a small, lone herdboy what he needed. His reply was, "I need a match."

One of our pastors, Rev. Lepeli Mpusi, was once a herdboy in the mountains. When he moved to the city to find work, he was invited to a tent meeting. There he heard the powerful message of salvation. He repented, and soon afterward attended the Church of the Bible Covenant Bible College. Now an ordained minister in the Church of the Nazarene, he is pastoring the first organized Nazarene church in Lesotho.

We are reminded that it only takes one match to get a fire burning or to light a lamp. I pray that we can be the match the Lord uses to bring warmth and the light of His love to the thousands of herdboys who need the gospel so desperately. There is little to brighten the lives of these young lads. Yet we know that the good news of Jesus Christ can change all that, giving these herdboys a future and a hope (see Jer. 29:11).

Reaching China Through the Mountain Kingdom

But you will receive power when the Holy Spirit comes on you; and you will be my witnesses in Jerusalem, and in all Judea and Samaria, and to the ends of the earth (Acts 1:8).

Jeff Jiang was born in Shanghai, China, in 1969. After finishing high school and technical school, he worked in a chemical factory for four years. He then worked in a French brewery in Bejing for two years. He came to Lesotho in 1994, where he worked for Nissan.

We met Jeff in February 1996 while he was working at a Nissan garage. He asked Dale to teach him the Bible, for he wanted to know about God. He had heard about Jesus in China from his girlfriend who was a Roman Catholic. Jeff knew the name Jesus and that He died on a cross, but he didn't know why Christ had died. He just knew that Jesus was a great man. Although people in China are not taught about God, Jeff took a course in Bible as literature at a university in Bejing in the mid-'90s.

What a joy to teach such an avid student!

After Jeff began Bible study with Dale, his heart was touched and understanding came. Watching Jeff during this time was exciting as the gospel of Christ became real to him, like watching a bud burst into full bloom.

Jeff was baptized in the Phuthiatsana River near HaMakhoathi and later joined the Church of the Nazarene there. Although he attended a church that spoke only Sesotho, he said, "I could not understand what they said, but I could feel the Spirit of God."

In 1997, Jeff took a survey course in the New Testament through an extension class. What a joy to

Jeff Jiang being baptized by missionary Dale Stotler and Pastor Malehlohonolo Seitlheko.

teach such an avid student! His grasp of the Scriptures was amazing. How we thank God for Jeff!

Jeff testified: "I accepted Jesus Christ and became a Christian, and He is very important to my life. Jesus is like a father, but much better than my earthly father. My father makes mistakes, but Jesus never makes a mistake. I enjoy life since I became a Christian."

When we went on furlough in July 1997, we wondered what would happen to Jeff, if he would still pursue his call to the ministry. When we returned to Lesotho a year later, Jeff told us he had written his father asking permission to attend Bible college, but his father said no. Jeff felt so compelled to go to Nazarene Theological College that he wrote his father again, telling him he was sorry to disappoint him, but he had made the decision to attend Bible school anyway. A few weeks later he received another letter from his father giving his blessing if that is what Jeff really wanted to do.

During the 1998 political crisis in Lesotho, Jeff witnessed the killing of several people. When the Chinese were especially targeted, most fled to Republic of South Africa. But Jeff stayed in the village, and the people protected and cared for him.

Jeff enrolled at Nazarene Theological College in the Republic of South Africa in February 1999. His dream is to finish Bible college and return to China to start a church in Shanghai. We are thankful God can use the Mountain Kingdom to reach China with the gospel—through Jeff Jiang.

Church Dedications in the Mountain Kingdom

by Deanna Banks

He [Solomon] will build a house for me [God]
(1 Chron. 17:12).

During our first four years in Lesotho, we had the privilege of seeing three churches started and buildings erected in the lowlands near Maseru: HaMakhoathi, HaNqosa, and Tsieng. We built the HaMakhoathi church with Alabaster funds. A Work and Witness team from South Weymouth, Massachusetts, and Alabaster funds built the HaNqosa Church. A Work and Witness team from the Pittsburgh District paired with Alabaster to build the church at Tsieng.

Since travel is expensive and most invited guests had a long distance to come, we planned all three dedication celebrations on the same weekend in November 1996: HaNqosa on Saturday morning, HaMakhoathi on Saturday night, and Tsieng on Sunday morning. Quite an undertaking, I might add.

In the Mountain Kingdom, any big celebration includes a feast. The menu? Pumpkin, beans, cabbage, and of course, mutton. We assigned each pastor to hunt for two sheep to be slaughtered for each church dedication. A farmer agreed to sell us sheep for M200 (U.S.$33) each. As time for the dedications neared, we went to Tsieng. Imagine Dale's shock when he used the rest room and found it a real mess. For fear that the sheep would be stolen, the pastor kept them locked in the toilet at night!

The following is an account of this weekend as seen through the eyes of a volunteer. Deanna wrote this letter to her Work and Witness teammates who had previously built a church in another area of South Africa.

I was invited to join some missionaries from Johannesburg who traveled to Lesotho one weekend. Dale and Pat Stotler had three churches to dedicate. I just happened to be there at the right time, as the contingent of fellow missionaries went to celebrate the dedications.

I had returned to South Africa as a volunteer, knowing and accepting that my visit to the village of Dan House would likely be my only opportunity to visit an African community. But here I was crossing the border into another country to participate in what has to be a significant milestone for a missionary—three of them! It would take a book for me to describe it fully. I will condense it.

First, the opportunity for fellowship with the missionaries was a delight for me. We traveled in one of the *combis* (small vans) and missionary Jaap Kanis's *bakkie* (little pickup). It gave me a chance to get better acquainted and to learn more from their perspective about the country and the work. As we approached Lesotho, the African landscape became more and more mountainous. It's a beautiful kingdom, though the capital city of Maseru, where the Stotlers live, is battle-scarred from the many uprisings and crimes. The Stotlers have experienced gunfire around their home, mortar projectiles overhead, and theft of their car. Their yard, of necessity, is double-fenced.

As we left the paved roads and traversed the muddy, rocky mountain paths to HaNqosa, we passed a man clad in his colorful Basotho blanket and rubber boots as he tilled his field behind an ox-drawn plow. The blanket served as a coat and pro-

The HaNqosa Church was built with Alabaster funds and a Work and Witness team from Massachusetts.

tected him against the rainy cold. The boots were protection against the snakes. Similarly dressed herdboys were also in nearby fields watching their charges.

In spite of the poverty, HaNqosa is a neat village of thatched-roofed *rondavels* and corrugated metal-roofed huts nestled into the side of the mountain. We drove through the village, over the crest of a hill, and found the church standing off by itself on a plateau. Beyond, there was nothing but the majestic mountains, fronted by a deep ravine.

I don't know what time the service was supposed to start, but we waited quite awhile as the people made their way from the village to the church. It was a miserable, rainy, cold day, but I will never forget the sight of the people walking over the crest of the hill to the church. They would come two, three, four at a time, wrapped in their blankets, some wearing boots (yikes! snakes around the church?), winding their way down the path toward the church. Though the crowd was small when we arrived, by the time the service was underway, there was standing room only.

Someone sang the first phrase of a song and the congregation joined in, singing in the unique, beautiful African harmony.

I never really knew when the service officially started. When enough people were there, someone sang the first phrase of a song and the congregation joined in, singing in unique, beautiful African harmony. That continued for quite some time. Eventually, one of the pastors took charge, and the service became more traditionally structured. I lost track of time, but we were there at least a couple of hours.

The church building was one large room with plank benches and two rooms with a separate entrance at the back. These rooms were intended for a parsonage. At the time, no one was living there, so they used the space to prepare and serve the meal that followed the service.

I had the impression we were going to bring our own food to eat on the road because of a tight schedule. When they announced the meal was being served and asked the audience to allow the guests to go first, I didn't think that meant us. But I found myself being ushered through the crowd toward the room where tables had been set for our use. To get there, we had to go through the room where the food was being served from large pots onto plates on the floor, which people were stepping over and around in mass confusion. Guess I was wrong! We were going to eat there after all!

I watched to see what the missionaries did. They just dove right in and started eating. I had been told we could safely eat anything that was cooked, but all I could think of was the water in which the food might have been cooked! Well, I gave it the old college try. Rice with a type of gravy, mashed potatoes with no gravy, peas, and some type of meat that was cold. I stuck with rice, mashed potatoes, and a few peas. In spite of my expressed willingness to "rough it," I wasn't anxious to spend the rest of my trip looking for nonexistent rest rooms while bumping over African roads! I ate enough to be polite but didn't exactly clean my plate. The unidentified meat turned out to be a sheep, which I understood had been penned up in an outhouse to keep it from getting away, then slaughtered for the meal. As someone accustomed to getting meat in neatly wrapped packages from a refrigerated case in supermarket, I still find the Lesotho way hard to comprehend.

Following the meal, we rode in shifts back to the paved road. Missionary Ina Kanis and I waited in the church for our turn. The people had eaten in the sanctuary, and the cleanup process was underway. Suddenly, an excited young lady rushed in from the "kitchen" to share a treat with a woman who was sitting a couple benches away from us. The younger one had two sheep's legs that had been cooked, and proudly held them up for the woman to see. They looked greasy, they bent at the joint as she dangled them, and I could see the forked hooves. The sight of those legs just about did me in! But they really must have been a treat. They were devoured—almost sucked dry—by the two women.

When we left, I rode in the cab of Kanises' pickup with them, a snug fit but more comfortable than the back of the truck! We fishtailed our way over the muddy, rocky road until we hit pavement and made our way to the next church at HaMakhoathi. The buildings and surroundings were more urban. They had rented chairs. No plank benches. Again, in time, there was standing room only, and the service was very similar.

A meal was served following this service also. This time, however, I was better prepared to handle the food. In both meals the veteran missionaries took good care of me, stopping me from absent-mindedly drinking the beverage one time and from

Tsieng Church being built by a Work and Witness team from the Pittsburgh District.

eating a cold salad another time. Either slip could have sentenced me to the rest room.

The next day was a bright, sunny Sunday. We dedicated the Tsieng Church, which the Pittsburgh District had built. Again, the building and surroundings were similar to the other churches, and the crowd was large.

In all three churches, I loved to observe the people, hear the singing, and sense the Spirit in the services. I know it was a thrilling time for the Stotlers, who have worked under oppressive circumstances to establish the church and bring the gospel to Lesotho.

As we made our way back to South Africa, we were caught up in the throngs of Lesotho residents who cross the border to earn a living in South Africa during the week. The long line at the customs office was slow-moving. The delay afforded an opportunity for the missionaries to point out to me a witch doctor, as evidenced by her attire and trappings, as she walked away from the line.

Lesotho. What a culture! What an experience! But what a special blessing from the Lord!

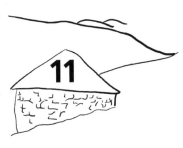

The Gospel's Power in the Mountain Kingdom

I am not ashamed of the gospel, because it is the power of God for the salvation of everyone who believes (Rom. 1:16).

High in the mountains in the interior of Lesotho are many river valleys. In one of these valleys sits the village of Manamaneng, meaning "Place of the Calves." Since Mission Aviation Fellowship (MAF) flies into these areas on a regular basis and knows the topography well, we consulted with Gary Toews, the MAF director in Lesotho at the time. We learned that this entire river valley with numerous villages had no active churches at all.

The government was in the process of building a health clinic, including an airstrip, in Manamaneng to provide basic health care. Since there are no roads into this area, travel by a 4x4 vehicle was not an option. The landing strip here is the highest in Lesotho at 2,310 meters (7,700 feet) above sea level. A plane can only land when the weather is favorable, and then with great care and an experienced pilot.

In Manamaneng and all of the mountainous regions, the people are extremely poor. Seventy percent of the schools in the highlands have no piped water, 50 percent have no latrines, and 30 percent have no desks or chairs. Teaching aids are almost nonexistent. One-third of all the teachers have no teaching certificates.

We soon learned that our idea of sanitation is a little different from theirs. We traveled to different villages for three days before we saw a toilet, which, by the way, was worth seeing. Painted bright red and blue and sitting on a prominent place in the village, it stood out in an otherwise drab landscape. Too bad it was an hour's swift walk from where we were staying.

On our first trip to Manamaneng, we simply wanted to assess the need, meet the chief, and secure permission to work in the area. Dale Stotler, Ntate Poly Seitlheko, and Ntate Lepeli Mpusi went together to "spy out the land." Upon their arrival, they found many people waiting at the clinic. The

Ntate Poly Seitlheko and Dale Stotler holding a service at Manamaneng.

people were actually a little disgusted, for they thought it was the doctor with Lesotho Flying Doctor Service coming to the clinic to see patients. Many had sick-in-the-tummy problems. (I wonder why!) The men offered to pray for all who were sick, so the people were a little happier. Every time they prayed for a group and opened their eyes, the line waiting to be prayed for had become a little longer. Finally, they finished.

As the ministers talked with the people, they learned that a woman had had a dream that, on the very day they were there, a white man and some Basotho pastors would arrive from Maseru to preach the Word of God. Word of this "dream" had traveled from village to village. Even without any electricity or phones, news still travels fast. Of course, with so little happening other than the ordinary task of keeping body and soul together, any news is welcome and important.

On this first visit, the chief gave the visitors a warm welcome. The "real" chief, Matete, works in the lowlands, so his wife is the acting chief. She is responsible for 16 villages. She graciously let us stay in her home during our three-day visit and gave us permission to work in all the villages under her jurisdiction.

The mountain people have so little, yet they graciously share what they have. Sometimes we'd just as soon they didn't share everything, such as the many little creeping critters. As outsiders, we learned the hard way how to deal with these unwanted creatures.

Over the next couple years, we flew into the area and began to establish a congregation. For almost a year, though, we were unable to get there because the dirt landing strip had deteriorated so much that Mission Aviation Fellowship could not land. In 1997 the government repaired the strip so the clinic could be finished and medical teams could again visit the mountain village.

On March 7, 1997, we left Maseru in hopes we could land at Manamaneng. The sky was overcast and stormy. But after some minutes of maneuvering around the thunderclouds, we flew high over the first few mountain ranges. After another 45 minutes, we landed safely on the newly repaired airstrip.

We waved good-bye to the MAF pilot, borrowed a horse to carry our supplies, and set out for the chief's village. Again, we had brought our food, bedding, and cooking gear for a week, plus a little extra in case the weather would not permit MAF to return when planned. All the supplies for the tiny shop in the village come from Pietermaritzburg, South Africa, about 150 kilometers (90 miles) away. They are brought by truck to the top of Sani Pass and then packed by horse or donkey into this area. We brought our own provisions, so what is in the shop would be available to the villagers.

**The chief wanted to show us
the site she had decided to
give us to build a church.**

After stopping in a village along the way and preaching to the 45 to 50 gathered there, we walked to the river and waded through it. After about an hour's time, we arrived at the chief's village, where she and the people joyously welcomed us. Each evening we held services in the chief's hut where we stayed. As we read and taught the Bible, the message touched the heart of the chief, and she wept. She, along with many others, requested prayer.

On this visit, the chief told us she had been waiting for us to return. She wanted to show us the site she had decided to give us to build a church. Before we asked, God answered. Not only did she offer us a field near her home, but also she offered the help of the village people to carry stone, sand, and water, or to do anything they could to help us build a church.

We were reminded of how much God loves us and especially the people in this forgotten area of Lesotho. As we see the light of God's Word penetrate the darkness of superstition, witchcraft, and ancestral worship, what a thrill it is to see lives changed! Where once there was a look of hopelessness and despair on their faces, now there is hope and joy and peace.

On certain days, we backpacked into neighboring villages to tell the people about Christ. Even though a village on the next mountain appears close, it often takes hours to hike that distance. In these mountain hamlets, the people knew nothing about Sunday School or church, so we spent much time teaching. On Friday and Saturday we visited the homes in Manamaneng and invited the people to come on Sunday morning to hear the Word of God. They came and sat on the hillside, listening intently to what we taught.

One Sunday Dale preached and the service closed at 1 P.M., but many people arrived so late and missed the message that they asked if we would begin again. We started all over for those who had just come. This service ended at three o'clock.

We left and went back to the chief's hut for a lunch of bread with a cup of tea. As we were eating, a little woman with a baby on her back came trudging up the path. She lamented, "Oh, I missed the service, I missed the service." We could see she was exhausted, so we gave her some bread and tea. Ntate Poly asked Dale to share with her what he had preached about that morning. Dale, instead, felt compelled to speak to her about the woman at the well in Samaria. As he spoke of the living water, she thumped her chest and said, "I have such joy at what you are telling me." Dale continued to speak, and she again interrupted him and said, "I have such joy and peace."

This little lady then said she must leave, as she needed to get home before dark. She pointed to her village. We could see it on the opposite mountain. Not very far, we thought. But she had walked three hours, wading across a wide river, to come and hear the Word of God. Without question, there is power in the message of the gospel.

A Wheelbarrow Offering in the Mountain Kingdom

A tithe of everything from the land, whether grain from the soil or fruit from the trees, belongs to the LORD; it is holy to the LORD (Lev. 27:30).

The concept of tithing is new for the Basotho people. Even those who have gone to some of the mainline churches have no idea what tithing means. This probably has to do with the fact that the country has survived for decades on foreign aid.

When we started the work in Lesotho, we knew the people must learn about tithing if the church would become self-supporting. Even the concept of pastoral support by the local church was new to them. Many of the churches in Lesotho survive on funds from selling used clothing or other items, such as mugs, shirts, and hats. Many are supported by outside organizations such as foreign mission boards. We want the Church of the Nazarene to be supported in the biblical way of tithes and offerings.

It is not unusual in Africa to have vegetables, a chicken, or a goat brought to church as tithe.

When the church at HaMakhoathi was started, we introduced the concept of tithing to the people. We were so pleased when Mr. Palea, one of the first converts, brought his tithe to church one Sunday in a wheelbarrow. He works for the chief and does not get paid in maloti, the local currency of Lesotho. He gets paid in the fruits of the harvest. In this instance, corn. He brought two 80-kilogram (175-pound) sacks of shelled corn and placed them in the front of the church. One sack was his tithe, and the other, a gift for the pastor. The "corn tithe" was sold, and the money put into the church funds.

It is not unusual in Africa to have vegetables, a chicken, or a goat brought to the church as tithe. The people may not have money, but they give of what they have. One day Rev. Lepeli Mpusi, pastor of Tsieng Church, brought his monthly report, and we saw that his tithes and offerings were over M3,000 (U.S.$500). We were so used to seeing M30-M100 (U.S.$5-$17) as tithes and offerings that we thought he had made a mistake. When we asked him about it, he told us the story.

Ntate Lerato, who works in the mines in the Republic of South Africa, tithes regularly. However, he contracted a chronic lung disease and was awarded a settlement of M30,000 (U.S.$5,000). When he came back to Lesotho on leave, he brought his tithe with him and put it in the offering that Sunday morning.

When so many of the Basotho miners have been retrenched, Ntate Lerato still works in the mines and is able to support his wife and children here in Lesotho. God does bless a cheerful giver. When our pastors were still with the Church of the Bible Covenant, Ntate's wife was saved. The pastors visited their home regularly, and Ntate was saved. Eventually they joined the Church of the Nazarene. They live across the Phutiatsana River from Tsieng, but they faithfully wade through the river each week to attend the Tsieng Church.

God's Gift of Grace in the Mountain Kingdom

I became a servant of this gospel by the gift of God's grace given me through the working of his power (Eph. 3:7).

'Me Eliza was from a poor family in the Butha-Buthe district. Her father died when she was young, and her mother raised the seven children. The St. John's Church she joined believes only in the Old Testament with the sacrifices, rituals, dreams, and visions.

'Me Eliza is actually the second wife of a man. Her husband's first wife left him with several children, ran off to the Republic of South Africa, eventually married another man, and had more children by him. The man, whom she had left, then married Eliza, who raised his children. Then he died.

Later, when the children's mother returned to Lesotho, they spurned 'Me Eliza, their stepmother. They said she was not their real mother even though she raised them from when they were young. They gave her no help at all. Today, this 70-plus-year-old woman goes to the fields to work as she has no other means of support. She lives on whatever she can raise.

'Me Eliza started attending the Church of the Nazarene at HaMakhoathi and was saved. She was baptized in the river at the 1998 Christmas Conference and joined the membership class. She is a sweet lady who radiates the love of God and testifies to God's faithfulness.

* * *

When she held the connected shells to her ear, she believed the spirit would tell her what was wrong with people.

'Me Maria was also raised in a mountain village in a poor family, but she moved to HaMakhoathi a long time ago. Originally a Roman Catholic, she changed to the St. John's Church and became a strong leader. Her whole family followed her example. Using the Old Testament as their basic doctrine, they made ritualistic sacrifices. Maria had many dreams and visions. She felt the "spirit" asking her to go to Durban on the seacoast, where she collected shells of various shapes to connect together. When she held the connected shells to her ear, she believed the spirit would tell her what was wrong with people. She went all around her town, praying for people by using ashes and holy water.

'Me Maria talked to the Nazarene pastor at HaMakhoathi one day and asked her to explain

'Me Eliza being baptized by Dale Stotler
and Pastor Malehlohonolo Seitlheko.

'Me Maria being baptized by Dale Stotler
and Pastor Malehlohonolo Seitlheko.

what the spirit had told her. The question concerned "putting off the old and putting on the new." Pastor Malehlohonolo explained that she needed to put off the old sacrifices and put on Jesus as the sacrifice for her sins. 'Me Maria believed and accepted Christ that day.

Today 'Me Maria has a vibrant testimony and is growing spiritually. She witnessed to her son, who also became a born-again believer. She and her son were baptized during the 1998 Christmas Conference. They attended the membership class, along with 'Me Eliza, and joined the Church of the Nazarene. In her mid-60s, 'Me Maria brings many people to church with her and testifies to everyone of God's power and grace.

'Me Eliza and 'Me Maria—two shining examples of God's gift of grace—are worth all of the investment in the Mountain Kingdom people.

Conflict in the Mountain Kingdom

*You will hear of wars and rumors of wars, but see to it
that you are not alarmed. Such things must happen,
but the end is still to come* (Matt. 24:6).

Peace. Yes, peace for a whole year. This was the message we heard when we returned from furlough in July 1998. The country's second general election in 40 years had taken place in May. The Lesotho Congress for Democracy (LCD) party had won by a landslide. Seemingly—and amazingly—the voting happened without any problems.

On August 4, 1998, in Maseru, the opposition parties staged a protest of the elections, stating there had been fraud. Demonstrators from the opposition parties camped outside the gates to the Royal Palace and vowed not to leave until the government was replaced with a coalition government. Loudspeakers were set up. Chanting and singing went on night and day for the next seven weeks.

On August 12 the demonstrators announced a nationwide stay-away from work. Thousands of young men and boys entered the city to enforce this protest strategy. They roamed the city in gangs of 100 or more, harassing and beating anyone who attempted to break the stay-away. This went on for a week. The next day, the police attempted to disperse the crowds in front of the palace by firing a tear gas canister. In the turmoil that followed, two policemen were shot and killed and 36 people were wounded by a grenade. The demonstrators planned for the stay-away to continue until the government toppled. However, the Lesotho Defense Force intervened, removed the barricades from the streets, and kept order so the people could go to work.

We awoke early one morning in mid-September to the sound of people celebrating in the city. We wondered what was happening and found out that the demonstrators had confiscated all government vehicles that entered the city center. They took them to the palace and impounded them in the palace grounds.

The opposition immediately and systematically looted and burned the businesses of the city.

The palace grounds looked like a used car lot. Even the city sewerage truck and government tractors were confiscated. The situation really deteriorated when factions within the army mutinied. Finally the prime minister requested help from the Southern African Development Countries (SADC), and on September 22 the SADC troops rolled across the border at 5 A.M. When the opposition found that the SADC had come, they immediately and systematically looted and burned the businesses in the city. The damage is estimated at U.S.$350 million. It will take years to rebuild what has been lost. All the confiscated government vehicles were set aflame also. The city was almost totally devastated.

When the protesters finished with Maseru, they went to other towns, looting and burning. People hauled away double beds and all kinds of furniture. One woman carried a refrigerator on her head and stopped about a kilometer from the center of the city and asked for a drink of water. Immediately after drinking, she fell on her face and died. People took so much that they lost things along the roads, and the roads were littered with stolen goods. Some people from other villages came with trucks and hauled goods away to be sold in their village shops. Weeks after the thefts and destruction, people would knock on our gate trying to sell goods obtained illegally. Sadly, a pharmaceutical factory was looted and burned, and we heard that at least 60 people died from ingesting stolen medicines.

At the beginning of 1999 it was quiet, but nothing had really been resolved. New elections are scheduled for 2000. As a result of this conflict, the people in the villages have become divided. One of our pastors said, "There is such hatred between people of the different political parties now that Satan is in control. Brothers are killing brothers, friends are killing friends. The hearts of the people are full of evil and have nothing good in them. All they think of is what bad things they can do to each other. Many people are hurt and angry about what has happened to their country because everyone is suffering now."

Yes, peace at last. But for how long? Will Lesotho always be in conflict? Only the peace of Christ in the hearts of people will bring lasting peace to the people of the Mountain Kingdom.

Devastation of Maseru

Shops looted and burned in the Mountain Kingdom

Epilogue

Working in Lesotho has been frustrating and challenging, yet exciting. In the time Dale and I have been here, we have seen the Lord do marvelous things. We realize more and more that it is not our work but God's. He will build His church as we are faithful to Him and sensitive to His leading. Despite all the turmoil in the country—coups, rumors of coups, police strikes, army mutinies, destructive war—God is changing lives.

During the recent turmoil, we lost track of Seeng Leuta, the released prisoner. However, on Christmas Sunday of 1998, she and her new husband arrived at the HaNqosa Church together. They live in a village about 7 kilometers (4.3 miles) from the church. She remains faithful to God, and for that we are thankful. The prison ministry continues to bear fruit.

God has blessed us with two ordained ministers and a lay pastor. Also, a young man, Mookameli, who feels called to the ministry, is taking class from Rev. Malehlohonolo through the Theological Education by Extension program. Mookameli comes from a village high in the mountains. We praise the Lord for him, for it is very difficult to find men and women who are willing to pastor in the mountains.

In the first four years of work in Lesotho, we established three congregations in the lowlands near the capital city of Maseru and several congregations in mountain areas. Our goal is to establish churches in the mountains, where there are very few organizations working to bring the gospel to the unreached people.

In February of 1999, the launching of the *JESUS* film provided another dynamic means for reaching the isolated people of the Mountain Kingdom. In the first two months, six showings to 6,426 people resulted in 1,277 new believers in Jesus Christ. We have trained 21 church members to show the film, and our goal—with the assistance of Campus Crusade for Christ and Mission Aviation Fellowship—is to start 25 new preaching points in the mountains within a year's time.

Indeed, the Mountain Kingdom enters the 21st century with political unrest, and yet the people battle with an even greater unrest—within their souls. Pray with us that the Church of the Nazarene shall be effective in its outreach both in the lowlands and in the mountains, *claiming Lesostho for Christ.*

Pronunciation Guide

The following information is provided to assist in pronouncing unfamiliar words in the book. The suggested pronunciations, though not precise, are close approximations of the way the terms are pronounced in English.

Adanech Biru	AH-dah-netch BIHR-oo
Addis Ababa	AD-uhs AH-buh-buh
Alfons	al-FAHNZ
Amharic	am-HAHR-ihk
bakkie	BAH-kee
balimo	bah-DEE-moh
Bantu	BAHN-too
Baphuti	bah-POO-tee
Basotho	bah-SOO-too
Boers	BOO-erz
Botswana	baht-SWAH-nuh
Butha-Buthe	BOO-thah-BOO-tay
Caledon	KAL-eh-dahn
combi	KOHM-bee
DoRego	doh-RAY-goh
Girmay	GER-may
HaMakema	hah-mah-KEE-mah
HaMakhoathi	hah-mah-KWAH-tee
HaNqosa	hah-nn-KOH-sah (The letter "q" is pronounced with the clicking sound used to get a horse to move faster.)
HaPopa	hah-POH-pah

85

Jiang	JANG
Katse	KAHT-see
Khotso-Pula-Nala	HOHT-soh-POO-luh-NAH-luh
kraal	KRAHL
Lepeli Mpusi	lah-PED-ee mm-POO-see
Lerato	lay-RAH-toh
Lesotho	luh-SOO-too
Letsenghatrae	let-seng-HAH-tray
Lumela Mme	DOO-may-lah MM-may
Lumela Ntate	DOO-may-lah nn-TAH-tee
Lumelang Boabuti	DOO-may-lahng boh-uh-BUH-tee
maloti	mah-LOH-tee
Malehlohonolo	MAH-lay-loh-hoh-NOH-loh
Manamaneng	mah-NAH-mah-neng
Mantsonyane	MAHNT-sahn-YAHN-ee
Marikabe	mah-ree-KAH-bee
Maseru	mah-SAY-roo
Matete	mah-TEE-tee
Mazioni	mah-zee-OH-nee
'Me Eliza	MM-may ee-LEEZ-uh
'Me Maria	MM-may mah-REE-uh
'Me Salomina	MM-may sahl-ah-MEE-nah
Molimo	moh-DEE-moh
Molimo Nthuse	moh-DEE-moh nn-TOO-say
Mookameli	moo-kah-MAY-dee
Moshoeshoe	moh-SHWEH-shway
Ntate Poly Seitlheko	nn-TAH-tee POH-lee say-TLAY-koh
Palea	pah-LAY-ah
Pietermaritzburg	pee-ter-MARH-ets-berg
Phuthiatsana	poo-tee-aht-SAH-nah
rondavels	RAHN-dah-vulz
sangomas	san-GOH-mahz

Sani	SAH-nee
Seeng Leuta	SEE-eng lay-OO-tah
Senqunyane	SEN-kuhn-YAHN-ee
Sesotho	seh-SOO-too
Thabo	THAH-boh
Tlhanyaku	tlahn-HAY-koo
Toews	TAYVZ
Tsieng	tsee-ENG
Tswana	SWAH-nuh
Vaal	VAHL
Yemen	YEH-muhn
Zulu	ZOO-loo